G000049361

THE LITTLE BOOK OF
QUEEN BEY

The wit and wisdom
of Beyoncé

THE LITTLE BOOK OF
QUEEN BEY

The wit and wisdom
of Beyoncé

First published in Great Britain in 2019 by Trapeze
an imprint of The Orion Publishing Group Ltd
Carmelite House, 50 Victoria Embankment
London EC4Y 0DZ

An Hachette UK Company

1 3 5 7 9 10 8 6 4 2

A CIP catalogue record for this book is
available from the British Library.

ISBN (Hardback) 978 1 4091 9164 3
ISBN (eBook) 978 1 4091 9165 0

Printed in Italy

MIX
Paper from
responsible sources
FSC® C023419

www.orionbooks.co.uk

CONTENTS

BODY POSITIVITY 7

EMPOWERMENT AND EQUALITY 23

MUSIC 43

CAREER 59

FAMILY AND FRIENDS 75

'IT'S A SILLY SONG, BUT IT'S NICE BECAUSE IT'S MADE CURVY WOMEN FEEL SEXY.'

ON BOOTYLICIOUS, *COSMOPOLITAN*
1 November 2006

'IT'S REALLY ABOUT WHO YOU ARE, AND THE HUMAN BEING, THAT MAKES YOU BEAUTIFUL.'

PEOPLE

7 May 2012

'I THINK IT'S IMPORTANT
AND MEN TO
APPRECIATE THE
IN THEIR

FOR WOMEN
SEE AND
BEAUTY
NATURAL BODIES.'

VOGUE
6 August 2018

'IT GETS EASIER TO BE CONFIDENT ABOUT MY BODY AS I GET OLDER.'

COSMOPOLITAN

1 November 2006

'I HAD ALL THE ICE CREAM I WANTED AND IT WAS THE HAPPIEST TIME OF MY LIFE.'

THIS MORNING
11 November 2008

'I DON'T KNOW WHAT IT
BUT MY DEFINITION IS

BOUNTIFUL,

SAYS IN THE DICTIONARY,
BEAUTIFUL,
AND BOUNCIFUL.'

ON BOOTYLICIOUS BEING INCLUDED IN THE DICTIONARY,
LATE SHOW WITH DAVID LETTERMAN
7 February 2006

'MY BIGGEST THING IS TO TEACH [BLUE]
NOT TO FOCUS ON THE AESTHETIC.'

PEOPLE
7 May 2012

'YOU CAN'T LET ANYONE TELL YOU WHAT YOUR BEST IS; YOU KNOW WHAT YOUR BEST IS.'

CNN
27 June 2011

'TO HAVE THE FREEDOM TO
AND NOT CARE ABOUT
OR FITTING INTO A
REALLY LIBERATING

LET GO OF ALL EGO,
WHAT I LOOK LIKE,
POPSTAR BOX, WAS
TO ME.'

CNN
27 June 2011

'I WANTED EVERYONE
THEIR CURVES,
HONESTY – THANKFUL FOR

TO FEEL THANKFUL FOR THEIR SASS, THEIR THEIR FREEDOM.'

ON HER COACHELLA PERFORMANCE, *HOMECOMING*
17 April 2019

'YOUR SELF-WORTH IS DETERMINED BY YOU.'

GQ MAGAZINE

10 January 2013

'DO WHAT YOU WERE BORN TO DO. YOU HAVE TO TRUST YOURSELF.'

COSMOPOLITAN

1 November 2006

'ULTIMATELY YOUR INDEPENDENCE
KNOWING WHO YOU ARE
HAPPY WITH

COMES FROM YOU
AND YOU BEING
YOURSELF.'

LIFE IS BUT A DREAM
16 February 2013

'IT IS SO LIBERATING TO REALLY KNOW WHAT I WANT, WHAT TRULY MAKES ME HAPPY, WHAT I WILL NOT TOLERATE.'

HARPER'S BAZAAR

11 October 2011

'HUMANITY REQUIRES BOTH MEN AND WOMEN AND WE ARE EQUALLY IMPORTANT AND NEED ONE ANOTHER.'

THE SHRIVER REPORT
1 December 2014

⚦

'I DON'T LIKE TO GAMBLE,
ONE THING I'M WILLING

BUT IF THERE'S
TO BET ON,
IT'S MYSELF.'

ABC NEWS
24 November 2009

'I'M VERY HAPPY IF

INSPIRE OR

SOMEONE WHO

AN OPPRESSED

MY WORDS CAN EVER

EMPOWER

CONSIDERS THEMSELVES

MINORITY.'

OUT MAGAZINE

8 April 2014

'I'M LEARNING THAT YOU CAN BE KIND AND BE STRONG BUT . . . I HAVE TO BE FAIR TO MYSELF.'

THE OPRAH WINFREY SHOW
11 November 2005

'IT'S IMPORTANT TO MAKE SURE YOU
HAVE YOUR OWN LIFE BEFORE YOU'RE
SOMEONE ELSE'S WIFE.'

THE OPRAH WINFREY SHOW
13 November 2008

'I FEEL LIKE WHENEVER SOMEONE
AND KINDA TAKES YOU OUT
USUALLY YOU'RE BETTER OFF

MAKES YOU FEEL **INSECURE** OF WHO YOU REALLY ARE, NOT AROUND THAT PERSON.'

MUCH
14 September 2006

'LESS THAN 100 YEARS AGO, WOMEN DID NOT HAVE THE RIGHT TO VOTE; LOOK HOW FAR WE'VE COME FROM HAVING NO VOICE.'

SPEAKING AT A HILLARY CLINTON RALLY, *CNN*

5 November 2016

'LGBTQI RIGHTS ARE HUMAN RIGHTS.'

GLAAD MEDIA AWARDS
28 March 2019

'IT WAS IMPORTANT TO
HAD NEVER SEEN THEMSELVES
LIKE THEY WERE

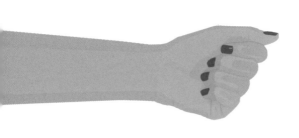

ME THAT EVERYONE WHO REPRESENTED FELT ON THAT STAGE WITH US.'

ON HER COACHELLA PERFORMANCE, *HOMECOMING*

17 April 2019

'I'VE ONLY SHARED WHO I AM THROUGH MY MUSIC AND I FEEL LIKE THAT MYSTIQUE IS VERY IMPORTANT.'

THE OPRAH WINFREY SHOW
11 November 2005

♫

'ONE OF THE REASONS I CONNECT TO THE SUPER BOWL IS THAT I APPROACH MY SHOWS LIKE AN ATHLETE.'

GQ MAGAZINE
10 January 2013

♫

45

TO HEAR IT MYSELF. HEAR THOSE SONGS REMIND US.'

ON FINDING OUR STRENGTH IN MUSIC, *MARIE CLAIRE*
6 May 2009

'I'M ATTRACTED TO SONGS THAT WILL BECOME A DINNER CONVERSATION!'

BILLBOARD
5 November 2011

'IN MY VIDEOS, I ALWAYS WANT TO BE A POWERFUL WOMAN. THAT'S MY MISSION.'

W MAGAZINE
1 July 2011

♫

49

'THERE'S MY PERSONAL LIFE, AND THEN ME AS SEXY AND

MY SENSITIVE SIDE,
A PERFORMER,
ENERGIZED AND FUN.'

THE NEW YORK TIMES
14 November 2008

'I ACTUALLY WENT AND BOUGHT TWENTY COPIES OF MY OWN RECORD.'

ON THE LAST THING SHE BOUGHT, *THE TYRA BANKS SHOW*
26 November 2008

♫

'SHE LOOKS UP TO PRINCE.'

ON SASHA FIERCE, *AOL SESSIONS*
13 October 2008

♫
53

'I WANTED TO SELL

AND I SOLD A

I WANTED TO

I WENT

A MILLION RECORDS,
MILLION RECORDS.
GO PLATINUM;
PLATINUM.'

ELLE
4 December 2008

'I KNOW I'M VERY PRIVATE, BUT I ALWAYS REVEAL MYSELF ON THE STAGE AND I ALWAYS REVEAL MYSELF IN MY MUSIC.'

AOL SESSIONS

13 October 2008

'IT'S FUN AND IT GIVES ME AN EXCUSE TO BLAME ANYTHING BAD ON SASHA FIERCE.'

THE ELLEN DEGENERES SHOW
25 November 2008

♫

CAREER

'I'VE BEEN WORKING NONSTOP SINCE I WAS 15. I DON'T EVEN KNOW HOW TO CHILL OUT.'

ELLE
4 December 2008

'I EMBRACE MISTAKES, THEY MAKE YOU WHO YOU ARE.'

YEAR OF FOUR
30 June 2011

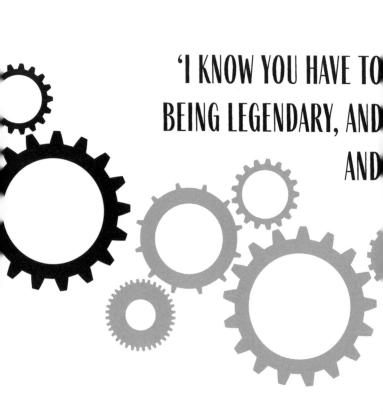

'I KNOW YOU HAVE TO
BEING LEGENDARY, AND
AND

MAKE A TRANSITION INTO

KNEW THAT IT WAS TIME.

I'M READY.'

THE NEW YORK TIMES
14 November 2008

'I LOVE MY JOB SO THE LEAST I
CAN DO IS GIVE MY ALL.'

THE ELLEN DEGENERES SHOW
25 November 2008

'I HAD TO SACRIFICE A LOT GROWING UP . . . AND I DIDN'T GET TO DO A LOT OF THINGS THAT MOST TEENAGE GIRLS DID.'

THE OPRAH WINFREY SHOW
13 November 2008

'THEY WANNA SAY IT'S BECAUSE

IT'S BECAUSE

OF THE SEXY CLOTHES . . . NO!
I'M TALENTED.'

NBC NEWS
8 July 2003

'THE OCEAN MAKES ME FEEL REALLY
SMALL AND IT PUTS MY WHOLE
LIFE INTO PERSPECTIVE.'

YEAR OF FOUR
30 June 2011

'I FEEL LIKE MY JOB IN THE INDUSTRY
IS TO PUSH THE LIMITS.'

BILLBOARD
5 November 2011

'I HOPE I CAN CREATE ART

ART THAT MAKES

OF

THAT **HELPS PEOPLE HEAL.**
PEOPLE FEEL PROUD
THEIR STRUGGLE.'

ELLE
4 Apil 2016

'IF EVERYTHING WAS PERFECT YOU
WOULD NEVER LEARN AND YOU
WOULD NEVER GROW.'

INTERVIEW
2 August 2001

'I WANTED TO FOLLOW IN THE FOOTSTEPS OF MADONNA AND BE A POWERHOUSE.'

CELEBRITY UNIVERSE
21 July 2014

FAMILY AND FRIENDS

'WE ARE BEST FRIENDS, WE GREW UP TOGETHER.'

ON DESTINY'S CHILD, *LATE SHOW WITH DAVID LETTERMAN*

7 February 2006

♡

'WE'VE BEEN TOGETHER SINCE I WAS
NINE YEARS OLD SO IT'S A FAMILY.'

ON DESTINY'S CHILD, *THE GRAHAM NORTON SHOW*

3 July 2003

'WE'VE LEARNED ABOUT LOYALTY, AND CARING ABOUT THE PEOPLE TOGETHER, **HOW TO BE** WHEN YOU'RE WRONG,

ABOUT THE IMPORTANCE OF LOVING IN THE GROUP, STICKING A **FRIEND**, HOW TO APOLOGIZE AND HOW TO COMPROMISE.'

ON DESTINY'S CHILD, *INTERVIEW MAGAZINE*
29 January 2013

'I LOVE MY HUSBAND, BUT THERE'S NOTHING LIKE A CONVERSATION WITH A WOMAN WHO UNDERSTANDS YOU.'

LIFE IS BUT A DREAM
16 February 2013

♡

'THE MAIN THING I'VE LEARNED IS NOT TO JUDGE PEOPLE.'

INTERVIEW MAGAZINE
29 January 2013

'SOME OF THE THINGS
DAUGHTERS – ALLOWING
EMOTIONS, THEIR PAIN AND
TO ALLOW AND SUPPORT
BOYS TO DO

THAT WE TEACH OUR
THEM TO EXPRESS THEIR
VULNERABILITY – WE NEED
OUR MEN AND
AS WELL.'

ELLE
4 April 2016

'WE'VE SHARED OUR BEST MEMORIES . . .
AND SOME OF OUR HARDEST MOMENTS.'

ON DESTINY'S CHILD, *THE OPRAH WINFREY SHOW*
15 November 2004

♡

'IT'S BEAUTIFUL TO SUPPORT EACH OTHER AND TO BE SECURE AND BE HAPPY FOR EACH OTHER.'

THE OPRAH WINFREY SHOW
15 November 2004

'IT'S GREAT TO KNOW THAT

AND THE HEELS AND I'M AT

I HAVE WARMTH

WHEN I TAKE OFF ALL THE MAKEUP

HOME - I HAVE A **LIFE**, AND

AND I HAVE **REALITY**.'

TODAY
9 February 2010

'MY MOTHER AND I ARE SO CLOSE AND I ALWAYS PRAYED THAT I WOULD HAVE THAT TYPE OF RELATIONSHIP WITH MY DAUGHTER.'

THE OPRAH WINFREY SHOW
16 February 2013

♡

'I'M JUST SO PROUD OF MY MOM . . . SHE LED ME BY EXAMPLE.'

ET CANADA

22 September 2011

♡

'BEING AROUND MY FAMILY KEEPS ME GROUNDED.'

TODAY
9 February 2010

♡

'SELLING A LOT OF RECORDS,
TO ME, IS NOT SUCCESS; HAPPINESS
IN MY PERSONAL LIFE IS SUCCESS TO ME.'

TODAY TONIGHT
31 July 2009

'AS THE MOTHER OF TWO
ME THAT **THEY**
TOO – IN BOOKS

GIRLS, IT'S IMPORTANT TO
SEE THEMSELVES
FILMS, AND ON RUNWAYS.'

VOGUE
6 August 2018

'I WANT MY DAUGHTER TO GROW UP SEEING A WOMAN LEAD OUR COUNTRY AND KNOW THAT OUR POSSIBILITIES ARE LIMITLESS.'

SPEAKING AT A HILLARY CLINTON RALLY, *CNN*

5 November 2016

♡

'WE HAVE TO TEACH OUR GIRLS THAT THEY CAN REACH AS HIGH AS HUMANLY POSSIBLE.'

THE SHRIVER REPORT
1 December 2014

♡